Shakespeare's Other Women

A New Anthology of Monologues

by Scott Kaiser

Muse of Fire Books

Muse of Fire Books
Ashland, OR 97520

ScottKaiserShakespeare.com

Cover image: Sappho (610–570 B.C.),
ancient Greek poet, depicted holding lyre
in a 19th-century engraving

Author photo: Jenny Graham

Editor: Amy Miller

Second Edition: 2018

Printed in the United States of America

In loving memory of
Catherine Coulson

INTRODUCTION

A New Anthology of Monologues

"What's a good Shakespeare monologue for women? One that isn't overdone at auditions?"

O, that I had a dollar for every time a young actress asked me that question!

The problem is, of course, that Shakespeare wrote a limited number of good speeches for women and they're all wildly overdone. You're never going to astonish a director with a speech they've never heard, because they've heard them all. Hundreds of times.

And while it's true that directors are looking for a unique interpretation of a speech, let's face it, it's a handicap. Because directors get tired. And their ears get numb. And they stop listening. Especially after a long day of sitting behind a table.

If you're a man, there are heaps of great speeches in the canon to choose from. There are princes and drunkards, scholars and clowns, soldiers and lovers of every age, disposition, and intelligence. But for a woman in search of a Shakespeare monologue, not so much.

What's an aspiring young actress to do?

Shakespeare's Other Women began as an attempt to address this ongoing dilemma—to provide young actresses with fresh possibilities when looking for a good Shakespeare monologue.

To accomplish this, I scoured the canon and asked: what are the great speeches that Shakespeare *might* have written for young women, but didn't? Then I set out to pen them myself—not in contemporary language, but the way the Bard himself might have composed them, using his vocabulary, his metrical art, and his rhetorical flair.

In the pages that follow, you'll find the results—an anthology of 36 brand new Shakespearean speeches for women. I offer them here as a gift to all the strong, intelligent, fearless young actresses out there searching for a good Shakespearean monologue to showcase their talents.

I hope you'll find them useful!

—Scott Kaiser

PRODUCTION HISTORY

Shakespeare's Other Women received a professional premiere production at the Island Shakespeare Festival in January of 2018 at the Whidbey Island Center for the Arts under the artistic directorship of Olena Hodges. The director was Erin Murray; the stage manager was Angelica Metcalfe; the set designer was David Gignac; the costume designer was Jody Harrison; the sound designers were Angelica Metcalfe and Olena Hodges; the lighting designer was Deana Duncan.

The cast was as follows:

Hero (*Much Ado About Nothing*), Beatrice, Venus, Dorcas	Libby Barnard
Joan, Juliet, Hero (*Mythology*), Nell (*Falstaff in Love*)	Francesca Betancourt
Katherine of Aragon, Imogen, Kate Keepdown, Rosaline (*Romeo and Juliet*)	Lexi Chipman
Hisperia, Dido, Leah, Emilia	Michelle Lynn Conklin
Mary Tudor, Audrey, Ophelia, Lucrece	Meghan Dolbey
Anne Boleyn, Nell (*The Comedy of Errors*), Margaret, Queen Elizabeth	Deana Duncan
Portia, Ariadne, Nemesis, Jessica	Aida Leguizamón
Titania, Calpurnia, Fulvia, Rosaline (*Love's Labor's Won*)	Kathryn Lynn Morgen
Hippolyta, Elizabeth Shore, Cleopatra, Lady Jane Grey	Isis Phoenix
John Heminges	.Jeff Allen Pierce
Henry Condell	G. Kent Taylor

Shakespeare's Other Women received an academic premiere production at Southern Oregon University in February of 2017 in the Stevenson Union Arena. The director was Scott Kaiser; the stage manager was Ada May; the scenic designer was Josephine Noel-Veatch; the costume designer was Rikki Condos; the sound designer was Reilly Schrader-Dee; the lighting designer was Michael Stanfill; the projection designer was Andrew Youngblood.

The cast was as follows:

Anne Boleyn, Imogen, Ophelia	Madeline Flemming
Portia, Elizabeth Shore, Nemesis	Hannah Fawcett
Joan la Pucelle, Ariadne, Nell (*Falstaff in Love*)	Meghan Nealon
Titania, Calpurnia, Fulvia	Katie Herling
Hero (*Much Ado About Nothing*), Audrey, Jessica	Lauren Taylor
Katherine of Aragon, Hero (*Mythology*), Emilia	Delaney Barbour
Hisperia, Nell (*The Comedy of Errors*), Dorcas	Jadi Dicksa
Hippolyta, Margaret, Rosaline (*Love's Labor's Won*)	Rachel Routh
Mary Tudor, Leah, Lady Jane Grey	Annie Murrell
Juliet, Cleopatra, Rosaline (*Romeo and Juliet*)	Samantha Miller
Dido, Kate Keepdown, Lucrece	Sarah Glasgow
Beatrice, Venus, Queen Elizabeth	Aurelia Grierson
Henry Condell	Erik Weiss
John Heminges	Karl Osladil
Women's understudy	Marie-Claire Erdynast
John Heminges understudy	Kyle Rispoli
Henry Condell understudy	Jake Raiter

Shakespeare's Other Women received an academic production at the University of Oklahoma in October of 2017 in the Gilson Lab Theatre. The director was Alissa Mortimer; the stage manager was Maria Doutey; the scenic designer was Anthony Wilkinson; the costume designer was Ciara Smith; the sound designer was Alex McSpadden; the lighting designer was Joshua Robbins.

The cast was as follows:

Anne Boleyn, Imogen, Ophelia	Caroline McCance
Portia, Elizabeth Shore, Nemesis	Kayla Booth
Joan la Pucelle, Ariadne, Nell (*Falstaff in Love*)	Madison Penzkover
Titania, Calpurnia, Fulvia	Madison Hill
Hero (*Much Ado About Nothing*), Audrey, Jessica	Maggie King
Katherine of Aragon, Hero (*Mythology*), Emilia	Grace Evans
Hisperia, Nell (*Comedy of Errors*), Dorcas	Kat Holland
Hippolyta, Margaret, Rosaline (*Love's Labor's Won*)	Alexis Ward
Mary Tudor, Leah, Lady Jane Grey	Alyssa Fantel
Juliet, Cleopatra, Rosaline (*Romeo and Juliet*)	Zoë Henson
Dido, Kate Keepdown, Lucrece	Carolyn Grundman
Beatrice, Venus, Queen Elizabeth	Hannah McNew
John Heminges	Julian Socha
Henry Condell	Micah Weese
Women's understudies	Sarah Harter Sierra Walker
Men's understudy	Nick Hone

THE PLAY IN BRIEF

It's 1623. Shakespeare's editors John Heminges and Henry Condell have finally finished assembling the Bard's *Complete Works*. But what to do with the surplus materials? Especially the unused women's speeches? *Shakespeare's Other Women* puts a spotlight on the women in Shakespeare who deserved to have more stage time, or even plays of their own. Featuring a large cast of women who inhabit dozens of strong female characters from Shakespeare, history, and mythology, the play presents 36 terrific new speeches that Shakespeare might have written for women, but didn't.

CHARACTERS

The Women (in order of appearance)

ANNE BOLEYN
PORTIA
JOAN LA PUCELLE
TITANIA
HERO (*Much Ado About Nothing*)
KATHERINE of ARAGON
HISPERIA
HIPPOLYTA
MARY TUDOR
JULIET
DIDO
BEATRICE
IMOGEN
ELIZABETH SHORE
ARIADNE
CALPURNIA
AUDREY
HERO (*Mythology*)

NELL (*The Comedy of Errors*)
MARGARET
LEAH
CLEOPATRA
KATE KEEPDOWN
VENUS
OPHELIA
NEMESIS
NELL (*Falstaff in Love*)
FULVIA
JESSICA
EMILIA
DORCAS
ROSALINE (*Love's Labor's Won*)
LADY JANE GREY
ROSALINE (*Romeo and Juliet*)
LUCRECE
QUEEN ELIZABETH

The Men

HENRY Condell
JOHN Heminges

PRODUCTION NOTES

PLACE and TIME

The printing house of John Heminges and Henry Condell, the co-editors of Shakespeare's First Folio, 1623. Numerous candles flicker on the projection screens upstage. A copy of Shakespeare's First Folio rests open on a pedestal at downstage center, bathed in a warm light.

PRODUCTION NOTES

As each new scene begins, a title to establish the location, and an iconographic image of that location, should be projected onto the set.

SET NOTES

Lightweight rehearsal blocks may be used by JOHN and HENRY throughout the performance to create chairs, benches, steps, beds—anything required by the action of the play.

COSTUME NOTES

Every woman in the cast should wear a similar base costume. As the women change from character to character, iconographic costume pieces and accessories should be added. But don't overdo it. Keep it simple.

PERFORMANCE NOTES

When a male scene partner is required by the monologue, JOHN or HENRY may be pulled into the scene to assume the role of the silent man, without altering or adding to their costumes. But they should never take focus. Not even for a moment.

SPEECH NOTES

No English accents are to be used to portray English characters. Ever. I mean it.

THE WOMEN

The number of women needed to perform the play is flexible. But every effort should be made to divide the monologues equally among the ensemble. No stars, please. And the monologues should be assigned in a way that provides each of the actresses enough time offstage to change costumes from one character to another. But you knew that.

THE MEN

HENRY is the chief editor of the First Folio and the brains of the printing house. He is intent on preserving Shakespeare's plays just as they were performed. He is Didi to John's Gogo.

JOHN handles the grunt work of the printing operation. He can barely read. He has an enthusiastic appreciation of all of Shakespeare's writing, whether it was performed or not. He is Gogo to Henry's Didi.

PROJECTIONS

Projected images should evoke the various locations noted throughout the script, beginning with the lit candles of the printing house. At times, we should see the shadows of the women silhouetted on the screens as they enter or exit the

space. The judicious use of that effect will enhance the final
moment of the play.

SOUND

Environmental sound may be used in certain scenes to evoke
locations. But don't overdo it. Soundscapes should never be
allowed to swamp the text.

MUSIC

Simon and Garfunkle's recording of "Scarborough Fair" is highly
recommended as preshow music, or some other composition
that elegantly straddles both 1623 and the present.

ACT ONE

[PROJECTION: A Printing House, London, 1623]

(Enter JOHN Heminges and HENRY Condell, admiring a copy of Shakespeare's First Folio, which rests open on a pedestal at downstage center, bathed in a warm light.)

HENRY
It's finished!

JOHN
It's beautiful!

HENRY
A spectacular achievement.

JOHN
The collected plays of William Shakespeare.

HENRY
All thirty-six plays.

JOHN
Thirty-seven.

HENRY
Thirty-six.

JOHN
Thirty-seven.

(HENRY counts from memory on his fingers, while JOHN counts from the title page of the Folio.)

HENRY	*(simultaneously)*	JOHN
Thirty-six.		Thirty-seven.

JOHN
Well...William would be proud.

HENRY
So proud.

JOHN
Well done, Henry.

HENRY
Well done, John.

JOHN
Nothing left to do then?

HENRY
Not a thing.

JOHN
To the tavern, then!

HENRY
To celebrate!

JOHN
Put out the lights.

HENRY
And then put out the lights.

(As they both enjoy the joke, JOHN carefully places the First Folio into a large box. In the process, he discovers another, smaller box inside.)

JOHN
Wait, what's this?

HENRY
What's what?

JOHN
This box.

HENRY
What box?

JOHN
This box.

HENRY
Oh! *That* box.

JOHN
What's in it?

HENRY
It's the superfluity.

JOHN
The super-what?

HENRY
The odds and ends.

JOHN
Okay...what odds and ends?

HENRY
You know, the deletions.

JOHN
Hmm...

HENRY
The scraps.

JOHN
Right.

(Pause.)

JOHN
What should we do with them?

HENRY
Not sure...toss them out?

JOHN
Maybe.

HENRY
Burn them up?

JOHN
Possibly...

HENRY
Hmm...

(Pause.)

JOHN
Can we take a look?

HENRY
If you like.

JOHN
Open it up.

HENRY
Sure.

JOHN
We'll just see.

HENRY
A quick peek.

(HENRY opens the box, removing a portfolio of handwritten papers.)

HENRY
Hmm...

JOHN
Quite a stack!

HENRY
I'd forgotten.

JOHN
Interesting...

HENRY
Hmm...

JOHN
What's this one?

HENRY
It's Anne Boleyn.

[PROJECTION: The Queen's Bedchamber, Greenwich Palace]

JOHN
From *The Life and Death of Queen Elizabeth*?

HENRY
That's right.

JOHN
Too bad he never finished that.

HENRY
Just as well.

JOHN
Why's that?

HENRY
Queen Elizabeth's mother? Beheaded? Onstage?

JOHN
Oh, right...not a good idea.

HENRY
Terrible...

JOHN
So this is...?

HENRY
Just after Elizabeth is born...

(We hear a baby crying in the next room.)

ANNE BOLEYN
I prithee, nurse, remove the child at once;
She troubles me. And leave me, all of you.
Alack, what shall I do? The King doth naught
But scowl since our Elizabeth was born.
He's choleric, impatient, sullen, rude,
And doth refuse to visit me in bed;
And yet, hath he not cause to scorn at me?
Did he annul his sacred marriage vows
To Spanish Katherine, defy the Pope,
And place me on the throne as his new Queen
To welcome to this world another girl?
Beshrew the day that his astrologers
Informed the King he should expect a son!
The sweetness of their honey promises
Begat in him these fits of bitter sorrow.
Now I do taste Queen Katherine's despair:
O'erthrown for failing to produce an heir!
Alas, I fear that Henry shall devise
Some sanctified excuse to cast aside
Another queen. In faith, till I present
His Highness with a living son and heir
My life as Henry's wife and England's Queen
Will never be secure, but fraught with danger!
I must entice him back into my bed.
But how? When his affections drive him to
Another woman in the royal court?
Unto Jane Seymore! My own maid-of honor!
The other day, in view of all my women,
He offered her a locket that contained
A miniature of himself. How dare the vixen

Consent to such a gift as I stood by!
I tore it from her hand with such a force
Her fingers bled, and like a child, she wept.
Indeed, she is a force to reckon with.
And yet, in order to survive, I must.
I'll send Elizabeth to Hatfield House,
And once more to my bed, I'll woo my spouse.

Exit ANNE BOLEYN.

JOHN
Who's that?

HENRY
It's Portia.

[PROJECTION: The Home of Portia and Brutus, Rome]

JOHN
From *The Merchant of Venice?*

HENRY
No, the other Portia...

JOHN
The other...?

HENRY
From *Julius Caesar*.

JOHN
Ah...

HENRY
The wife of Brutus.

JOHN
Yes...

HENRY
The speech he cut...

JOHN
Where she's spying on her husband...?

HENRY
Exactly...

JOHN
While he meets with the conspirators...

HENRY
Yes...

JOHN
As they plot the assassination of Caesar...

(JOHN stands at attention to become Lucius.)

PORTIA
How now, good Lucius? Tell me, who is here?
What visitors do gather in our orchard
To murmur with thy gentle master Brutus
At this unhallowed hour? I prithee, speak.
There is some weighty business here at hand
To be enshrouded thus in secrecy!
I saw them enter through the orchard gates,
Like gliding ghosts emerging from their graves.
Pray, tell me, Lucius, wherefore this assembly?
What guilty purpose brings them to our house
Concealed in darkness? Fie, wilt thou not speak?
Good troth, you men! Last night, my husband, too,

Mistrusting of my sex, refused to speak,
For fear I might divulge, upon the rack,
Intelligence which cannot be unheard.
How shall I prove to Brutus he may trust
My flesh to be as dauntless as my spirit?
That lashes, wheels, and fire cannot inflict
Upon this body cruelty sufficient
To make my tongue betray his confidence.
What evidence shall speak of my resolve?
My loyal Lucius, fetch the barber's blade
From Brutus' chambers. Nay, be not afraid.
A sharpened knife shall honorably serve
To purchase me the trust that I deserve.
I'll cut a gash along my naked thigh
That shall my husband's doubts in me belie;
For if he will not trust me with his life,
'Twere better to be dead than Brutus' wife.

Exit PORTIA.

JOHN
What have you got there?

HENRY
It's Joan la Pucelle.

[PROJECTION: A Field in Domrémy, France]

JOHN
Who?

HENRY
Joan la Pucelle.

JOHN
Joan of Arc?

HENRY
If you prefer.

JOHN
From *King Henry the Sixth, Part One?*

HENRY
No, from *The Life and Death of Joan la Pucelle.*

JOHN
Really?

HENRY
An earlier draft.

JOHN
Oh, okay...

HENRY
It's the scene where the Virgin Mary appears to Joan in the
fields...

JOAN LA PUCELLE
Yet, Holy Mary, stay! How can this be?
I do not understand thy Heavenly intents:
How can I be anointed by your Grace
To free all France from her calamity?
For I am just a girl, a shepherdess,
A virgin like yourself, a simple maiden,
Obedient and humble as the lamb.
Alack, I know not, I, the blood-stained field,
But only fields bestrewn with grazing sheep,
And even they will barely heed my call
When I entreat them follow at my heels.
How might I outface mighty armies then?
Disarm brave soldiers, vanquish generals?

I shall be mocked, or cast aside as mad,
Or worse, marked for the gallows as a fraud,
A wolvish traitor to my loving country.
Alack, I am unworthy of this duty,
Unfit and undeserving of the trust
That your celestial holiness hath placed
Upon my shoulders, powerless to render
The miracles that you require of me.
I do beseech thee, therefore, on my knees,
Ordain another mortal better poised
To be the savior of France, a soul
More fit than I to undertake this deed,
Whose maiden blood knows naught but how to bleed.

(We hear churchbells ringing in the distance, which JOAN receives as Mary's answer.)

Exit JOAN LA PUCELLE.

HENRY
You'll remember this one.

JOHN
Who is it?

HENRY
It's Titania.

[PROJECTION: A Forest Outside Athens]

JOHN
Ah! From *A Midsummer Night's Dream.*

HENRY
No...

JOHN
No?

HENRY
No. It's from *Titania, Queen of the Fairies.*

(We hear wind chimes.)

JOHN
Oh...the prequel, right?

HENRY
Right...so this is Titania mourning the death of her votaress...

JOHN
Her votaress?

HENRY
Yes, her human attendant, Belinda...the lady who died giving
birth to a boy?

*(TITANIA hands a newborn baby in swaddling clothes to JOHN,
who hands it back later, when beckoned.)*

JOHN
The little boy that Oberon wants for himself?

HENRY
Exactly...

TITANIA
My fairest votaress, my sweet Belinda!
Though human, I shall miss thy company,
For thou didst know the way to make me merry.
Alas, how tragic to be born a mortal,
To be composed of flesh and blood and bone,

And subject to that king of tyrants, death,
Yea, even in the throes of giving life!
In this your favorite grove I've buried thee,
Amongst the flowers that you so adored:
These hawthorn trees shall be thy canopy,
This bank of wild thyme, thy timeless bed,
This mound of nodding violets, thy pillow.
Your son, the name of Umbriel I'll give,
And for thy sake, I'll raise him as mine own,
And he shall live with me amongst the spirits
That do inhabit these Athenian woods.
But, O, my sweet Belinda, my heart grieves
To think thou didst with lies requite my love,
For often you did claim an Indian King
Was father to this child. But now, 'tis plain
The boy's a halfling, not a human mortal,
The offspring of a fairy, not a man.
And yet, methinks, his father was a King,
For well I know his eyes, his lips, his cheek.
Why, he's the very glass of Oberon!
Unfaithful wretch! Disloyal Oberon!
Didst thou seduce Belinda with thy charms,
Enticing her into thy flowery bed?
O Fairy King, I have no doubt 'tis so!
But I'll not tell thee of my deep suspicions,
Nor give thee access to this little prince.
Yea, Oberon, I'll keep thy son from thee
To punish thee for thy disloyalty!

Exit TITANIA.

JOHN
Who's next?

HENRY
Hero.

[PROJECTION: The Home of Leonato, Governor of Messina]

JOHN
Hero...?

HENRY
The young daughter of Leonato, the governor of Messina?

JOHN
Oh, yes...from *Much Ado About Nothing.*

HENRY
No, this is from *Beatrice and Benedick.*

JOHN
Oh, I loved that play!

HENRY
As did I...

JOHN
I begged him to finish that!

HENRY
We all did...

JOHN
So this is...?

HENRY
Right after Hero meets Claudio for the first time...

JOHN
Right...

HENRY
Before all the men go off to war...

JOHN
Yes...and she's already falling for him...

HERO
Most noble Claudio! My father says
Thou art a count, and I do well believe him.
O bounteous count! Most fortunate encounter!
What? Shall I count thee now among my friends?
Or shall I count the number of sweet words
That passed thy lips to enter in mine ear?
Or count the glances that our greedy eyes
Did steal, and then return? Or shall I count
The world of sighs that from my breast shall fly
Until I do encounter thee again?
Or count the burning kisses yet to come?
Ay, me! I'll count myself a woman bless'd
If thou wilt have me as thy loving wife!
The countess Hero! Countess to a hero!
How many countless days must I endure
Till then? How many countless nights hold out?
Ay me! I shall be counted as a fool
To fall so deep in love upon so slight
An interchange of eyes. O feeble flesh!
I must needs hold thee to account if thou
Wilt give away my heart with such abandon!
And yet, how shall I counterfeit indifference?
Alack, how many countless maidens, Cupid,
Hast with thine amorous arrows likewise struck?
A single one pursued by countless zeros!
Then count me now among thy fallen heroes!

Exit HERO.

JOHN
Who have you got there?

HENRY
It's Katherine of Aragon...

JOHN
The first wife of King Henry the Eighth?

HENRY
Yes, but this is from *King Henry the Seventh.*

[PROJECTION: The Private Chambers of King Henry VII]

JOHN
Henry the Seventh?

HENRY
Right, when Katherine was just a young woman...

JOHN
Oh, yes, I remember! First, she was married to Prince Arthur...

HENRY
Right! Henry the Eighth's older brother...

JOHN
The sickly teenager who dies...

HENRY
You've got it.

JOHN
So....?

HENRY
So...Henry the Seventh asks Katherine if she's carrying
Arthur's child...

JOHN
Hoping for an heir to the throne...

KATHERINE of ARAGON
My gracious sovereign, I would to God
I could to thee impart I am with child
By my late husband Arthur, thy dear son,
Whose sudden death hath pierced my very heart.
But yet I must confess, in sight of heaven,
I am the thing I was when I first came
Unto your royal court from Spain, that is,
A true, unsullied maid, untouched of man.
Though true it is the Prince and I did share
A single bed upon our wedding night,
Our sleeping chamber blessed by rev'rend bishops
That our most sacred union might bear fruit;
Yet, when these holy rites did reach an end,
And that the Prince and I were left alone
Behind the curtains of our nuptial bed,
Young Arthur never pressed a groom's delight
In his new bride, nor sought to satisfy
His royal duty to produce an heir.
And though the Prince at break of day did boast—
Alas, my lord, I blush to speak of it!—
Of thirsty work, and lusty aims fulfilled,
I swear to thee, your grace, by all that's holy,
Our marriage vows were never solemniz'd
By that most intimate of acts that binds,
In sight of God, a husband to a wife.
Thereafter, we did share a single bed,
Six nights, or maybe seven, altogether,
Yet, I shall swear, until my final hour,

He never set a hand upon my person.
My duenna did attend me on those nights
And will, by oath, confirm this to be true,
For she did witness all that did ensue.

Exit KATHERINE of ARAGON.

HENRY
You'll like this one...

JOHN
Who's this?

HENRY
Hisperia.

[PROJECTION: The Court of Duke Frederick]

JOHN
Hmmm...never heard of her...

HENRY
From *As You Like It?*

JOHN
Hmmm...

HENRY
She's a waiting gentlewoman to Celia...

JOHN
To Celia...?

HENRY
Celia...Rosalind's best friend?

JOHN
Ah...

HENRY
So, Rosalind and Celia have gone missing...

JOHN
Right...

HENRY
Because they've run off to the forest of Arden...

JOHN
Yes...

HENRY
And a Lord of the court asks Hisperia if she knows anything...

*(HISPERIA folds a load of laundry from a basket, placing the folded
items in HENRY's arms.)*

HISPERIA
Why ask you this of me? 'Tis not my trade to spy upon my
mistresses and buzz their every doing to the Duke. I am a loyal
servant, I, and know the way to keep a conference. Nay, Duke
Frederick shall not hear from me how Rosalind and Celia went
to bed at their appointed hour, and how at dawn those beds
were cold and restless. I am no backstairs tell-tale, I. He shall
not hear from me how his daughter and her cousin did much
commend the parts and graces of the handsome man that
did lately throw down Charles the wrestler, for that is not my
calling, nor his business. Nor shall he hear from me 'tis rumored
'mongst the waiting-gentlewomen that wherever those two
maidenheads have gone, that much-admired youth is surely in
their company, for I do scorn such savory employment. Nor
shall he know from me how their incontinent companion, the

knavish Touchstone, is also nowhere to be found within the court, for such handiwork is too base for my vocation. Be gone then, fool, for I do know the way to tame my tongue, and thou shalt never learn a whit from me!

(She takes the folded pile of laundry from HENRY, and places it back in her basket.)

Exit HISPERIA.

JOHN
Who's next?

HENRY
It's Hippolyta.

JOHN
Oh! From *A Midsummer Night's Dream.*

HENRY
No, from *Hippolyta and Theseus.*

[PROJECTION: A Battlefield in the Amazon]

JOHN
Wait, what?...Is that..?

HENRY
The prequel.

JOHN
Ah!...So Hippolyta is...

HENRY
The Queen of the Amazons.

JOHN
Oh, yes...she's defeated in combat by Theseus...

(We hear the sound of swordplay offstage, which ends in a bind and a disarm.)

HENRY
Correct...

JOHN
And that's how they fall in love!

HENRY
Indeed.

HIPPOLYTA
How now? Why dost thou pause, brave Theseus?
Thou hast disarm'd me with thy matchless sword
And laid my body bare to thine assault.
Believe me, man, had I so injured thee,
And did in hand possess thy piercing steel,
I would not pause for leaden contemplation
But would, as any warrior, strike home.
Why dost thou cease thy merciless advance?
Wherefore these gentle looks of charity?
Ay me! Dost thou intend to add my name
To thy beswollen catalogue of conquests?
Yea, I do know of thy proud triumphs, Theseus:
Of beauteous Helen, she whom you abducted,
When she was but a tender youth, from Troy;
Of Perigouna, she whose father, Sinnis,
You put to death that you might ravish her,
By whom you have a son, young Melanippus;
Of Ariadne, she who guided you
From forth King Minos' labyrinth with string,
Whom thou didst cunningly forsake upon

The Isle of Naxos for the love of Aegle;
These labors infamous and many more,
Yea, more than any author may set down,
Fill up the shameless pages of thy spoils.
And hast thou pricked me down in thy vast book
As one of those sad maids to be subdued
For thy amusement? Ravish'd, then forgotten?
If this be thy intent, bold Theseus,
Be merciful, and strike me down at once!
For I would rather perish on thy sword
Than die in thy embrace with pangs of love!
Yea, thrust the fearful shaft into my heart
And vanquish me, for well I know thine art.

(We hear a heavy broadsword being sheathed.)

Exit HIPPOLYTA, as if following Theseus.

JOHN
What's that one from?

HENRY
It's from the *Tragic History of Queen Mary*.

[PROJECTION: A Bedchamber in the Royal Palace of Queen Mary]

JOHN
Ah yes, *Bloody Mary*.

HENRY
Yes.

JOHN
What's the speech?

HENRY
That time Queen Mary thought she was pregnant...

JOHN
Right...I remember...

HENRY
She gained weight and felt nauseous for months...

JOHN
But she wasn't pregnant at all?

HENRY
No, she wasn't...

(HENRY becomes Mary's doctor, and JOHN his assistant.)

MARY TUDOR
I prithee, leave me, doctor! Go, at once!
Yea, all of you! I must needs have my rest.
What said the fawning villain? Not with child?
Conceived of my o'erripe imagination?
Alack! My shame shall travel far and wide,
And my good name, in every alehouse, mocked;
My enemies shall revel and rejoice,
Crying, "The Queen hath given birth to wind!"
Ay me! How shall I tell these news to Phillip,
Who longs to lead his armies against France?
For when he learns there is no royal heir,
No son of his own blood to claim the throne,
I shall be left alone to roam the palace
With no companion but mine own despair.
O God above, why dost thou persecute
Thy faithful servant Mary with this trial?
Must I, upon my death bed, countenance
Elizabeth, my Protestant half-sister,

The daughter to that strumpet Anne Boleyn,
Succeeding me as Queen, to break with Rome,
And reassert my father's Popeless church?
Marry, I see this is thy punishment
For having tolerated heretics
To flourish in my realm. But how shall I
Redeem myself before thee, dear Redeemer?
I shall command the enemies of god,
Upon the holy altar, to renounce
All loyalty unto the Church of England.
They shall, 'fore God, their heresies forsake,
Or, for their sins, I'll burn them at the stake.

Exit MARY TUDOR.

HENRY
Here's another one you'll like.

JOHN
Who's that?

HENRY
That's Juliet.

[PROJECTION: A Home in Vienna]

JOHN
Ah, from *Romeo and Juliet*.

HENRY
No, from *Measure for Measure*.

JOHN
Huh? There's no Juliet in *Measure for Measure*.

HENRY
Yes, there is. Remember? Isabella's brother, Claudio...

JOHN
Yes...

HENRY
Gets his girlfriend pregnant...?

JOHN
Oh, right...

HENRY
Which is why Angelo sentences Claudio to death...?

JOHN
Yes, I remember...

HENRY
So Juliet's the pregnant girlfriend.

JOHN
Ah!

(When beckoned, JOHN goes to JULIET and becomes Claudio.)

JULIET
Come hither, love. Canst feel him? There! A foot!
He knocks upon the doorway of this world
For that he longs to see his father's face.
O, my dear Claudio! What shall we do?
We must make room for this our budding child,
That every day doth make his presence known
By pushing out the walls of his small cell
And setting up fresh lodgings in my heart.
O Claudio, no longer may we hide

Our errant love with flowing drapery,
With little lies, and flowery inventions!
No longer may we secretly defy
The strong objections of my willful father,
Whom to our union never will consent
Until his second childishness doth come!
Nor do I now believe that we shall see
The ample dowry that was well assured
By my enfeebled grandam in the east;
I prithee, therefore, gentle Claudio,
If thou dost love me, let us wed at once,
This very night, or if not, then tomorrow,
Or if not on the morrow, then the day
That follows thereupon, but soon, my love!
Or if not so, then let us leave Vienna
And travel to a place that knows us not;
To Prague, where I do hear the Emperor
Doth rule his city with a tolerance
And wisdom that doth make his name belov'd
Among his people. Yet, whate're we do,
Sweet Claudio, let's do it suddenly!
O let us in this state no longer stay,
For trouble finds us if we make delay.

(JULIET takes Claudio's hand, leading him towards an exit...)

Exit JULIET.

HENRY
Oh, yes...

JOHN
What's that?

HENRY
It's from *Dido and Aeneas.*

[PROJECTION: The Palace of Queen Dido in the City of Carthage]

JOHN
Dido, the Queen of Carthage?

HENRY
Yes, and Aeneas, the Trojan warrior.

JOHN
Right, the gods hook them up...

HENRY
And they have a hot fling...

JOHN
For about a year!

HENRY
But then Aeneas sneaks away one night...

JOHN
And sails off to Italy!

(We hear the ocean.)

HENRY
Leaving Dido behind...

DIDO
Alack, 'tis true! He's gone! Aeneas, gone!
Mine eyes cannot persuade my trusting heart
To view this spectacle of treachery.
And yet, 'tis true! O see, thou stubborn heart!
The Grecian fleet hath turned its back upon
The harborage of Carthage, sailing north

To seek out fruitful ports in Italy.
O heartless, cruel Aeneas! Faithless wretch!
How could'st thou steal away without a word?
Without a last embrace? Without a kiss?
O break, my mortal heart! I prithee, split
In two, and nevermore be heard to beat!
O, false Aeneas, now I curse the day
You e'er set foot upon the shores of Carthage!
I curse myself for giving you good welcome,
For offering to take you as my lord,
To share with you my bed, my life, my kingdom!
O hear, great Neptune, Dido's mortal pleas:
I prithee, blast these haughty Grecian ships
And swallow them beneath the ruthless waves!
Great Mars, be now my champion and defense,
For I do here proclaim perpetual enmity
'Twixt Carthage and the progeny of Troy!
My loving sister, Anne, summon my servants.
Bid them convey the bridal bed whereon
Aeneas and myself hath lain together,
Yea, all the weapons, clothes, and moveables
That, in his heedless haste, he left behind,
And have them set atop a wooden pyre
To be erected here upon the beach,
That I may set ablaze all evidence
Of his vile presence in my royal palace.
(*Aside*) Atop that pyre, I shall, with my first gift,
My lover's sword, impale my lover's heart.
My soul, Aeneas, soon shall follow thee,
To venge the evil you have done to me.

Exit DIDO.

HENRY
Remember this?

JOHN
What have you got there?

HENRY
It's from *Beatrice and Benedick*...

[PROJECTION: Governor Leonato's House, Messina]

JOHN
Oh, good!

HENRY
So, this is Beatrice...

JOHN
In the middle of the night...?

HENRY
Yes...

(We hear crickets.)

JOHN
When Benedick tries to sneak away...?

HENRY
Yes...

JOHN
But she catches him in the act!

(HENRY sits down to become BENEDICK, and begins "pulling on" his boots.)

BEATRICE
What? Wilt thou leave me thus without a word?

Steal from my bed before the break of day
Without a parting kiss? A fare thee well?
O Benedick! Did we not, by the moon,
Dear heart, a hundred eager kisses share,
A thousand sighs, ten thousand fervent oaths
To lie together till we lie no more,
And wilt thou, signor, like a tim'rous thief,
Withdraw in barefoot silence from my chamber
While I do lie asleep? In cowish terror
Sound a retreat after the field is won?
Fly the enemy after the surrender?
Alas, how many foolish, doting women,
With that intoxicating tongue of thine,
Hast thou, like Beatrice, made drunk with love?
What, no defense, good sir? No quick repost?
No quips? What, not a syllable of wit?
Hath all the bullets of thy brain been spent?
Then, come thy ways; I shall examine thee
As one that I have taken prisoner:
Say, dost thou love me? Yea, I know thou dost!
Confess it, love, and I shall show thee mercy.
Great Mars, wilt thou not say so much? Ay, so.
Then, mount thy halting horse, good Signor Jest,
And ride apace to war! Trumpet the charge
And dart thy wit upon the enemy,
Where it shall vex them into apoplexy,
And spare the innocent. O Benedick!
From this day forward to the end of days,
I nevermore shall trust thy faithless ways!
Now get thee hence, to war! And by God's feet,
I swear that any man you kill, I'll eat!

Exit BEATRICE.

JOHN
What have you got?

HENRY
This is Imogen.

[PROJECTION: The Palace of King Cymbeline of Britain]

JOHN
From *Cymbeline?*

HENRY
No, from *Princess Imogen.*

JOHN
Ah, yes, the prequel...

HENRY
Yes, a speech from the fourth act...

JOHN
The elopement scene?

HENRY
Yes, where she plots her escape from the court...

(We hear leaves rustling in the wind, and a creek trickling in the distance.)

JOHN
To marry her lover, Posthumus...

HENRY
Yes...

JOHN
Without the King's consent?

HENRY
Exactly...

IMOGEN
My dearest Posthumus, my dear, dear lord,
Whom I do cherish more than mine own life,
More than my liberty, mine honesty,
More than all mores my tongue may yet devise,
Although it will incur the regal wrath
Of my tempestuous and stubborn father,
Let us be wed this very day, my love!
This morning or this afternoon, or else
This evening, or tomorrow at the latest,
But now, without delay! Pisanio,
Your trusted servingman, shall be employed—
Though yet I know not how—to bring about
A swift and binding union 'twixt us twain
Beyond the compass of the royal court!
And therefore, let us go at once, my love,
No matter where, for if, by Sunday next
We be not bound as one by holy oath,
I must be married to that clotpole Cloten,
The halfwit son begotten of the queen,
My father's new-made wife. Alack the day
That he did knit his soul to such a monster!
Is he so hot that he cannot perceive
The wintry ice that flows within her veins?
And such a son! I'd rather have this head
Dissevered from these shoulders, or these limbs,
By some abhorrent beast, torn from this trunk
Before I would take hands with such a fool!
What sayst thou, love? Dost thou consent to this
My sudden scheme? Sweet Posthumus, say ay,
And I will love thee faithfully and true
Though Jupiter himself should urge delay
And frown upon our secret wedding day!

(IMOGEN extends her hand, beckoning Posthumus to follow her...)

Exit IMOGEN.

JOHN
And this is...?

HENRY
Elizabeth Shore.

JOHN
And she was...?

HENRY
King Edward the Fourth's mistress.

[PROJECTION: The Royal Chambers of King Edward IV]

JOHN
King Edward's mistress...

HENRY
You know...from *Richard the Third?*

JOHN
Oh! Jane Shore! The one they called a witch and a whore?
Everyone hated her, right?

HENRY
Right, because she had a powerful influence over the King. But
she was a peacemaker, actually...

JOHN
Really?

HENRY
That's true.

JOHN
So what's happening here?

HENRY
So, King Edward is dying, and everyone is squabbling, and
Elizabeth is imploring the King to make peace between the
families before it's too late...

(HENRY sits down to become King Edward.)

ELIZABETH SHORE
I speak not for myself, my valiant Edward,
But rather do I sue for thee, my love;
For thy dear sake, and for thy legacy,
Do I suggest this prudent course of action.
Your health declines apace, and time is brief
To make amends and set affairs aright.
If thy immortal soul will enter heaven,
You must on earth make lasting peace among
The members of your factious family,
Betwixt the stubborn nobles of the Woodvilles,
And kinsmen loyal to the house of York.
I prithee, Edward, summon them this day,
Collect them all together in one room
And bid them pledge their faith to one another;
Yea, if they love thee, as they swear they do,
Let them embrace and shake each other's hands,
And vow to set aside all enmity,
And turn all thoughts of harm to perfect love.
But most of all, I do beseech thee, Ned,
To pardon instantly thy brother George,
Now wrongfully imprisoned in the Tower,
For any man of honesty and wisdom,

Yea, any man of judgment may perceive
That weak surmises and false prophecy
Condemn'd his body to that fearful place,
Not evidence of treachery in him;
And for I know thy gentle soul will mourn
If any injury should come to him
While under thy strict edict he doth suffer,
I prithee pardon him, and pardon all,
Lest to a fiery place thy soul shall fall.

Exit ELIZABETH SHORE.

HENRY
This looks familiar.

JOHN
What is it?

HENRY
Well...it seems to be from *Theseus*.

[PROJECTION: Before the Labyrinth of Minos, in Crete]

JOHN
The Adventures of Theseus of Athens?

HENRY
That's the one.

JOHN
Oh, I liked that one! So much action...

HENRY
And romance...

JOHN
Yes...

HENRY
So this is Ariadne.

JOHN
The daughter of the King of Crete...

HENRY
King Minos, yes....

JOHN
Who oversees the famous labyrinth...

HENRY
Yes, that's right...

(HENRY kneels to become Theseus, while JOHN becomes a guard, holding a ball of string behind his back, which he hands to ARIADNE upon demand.)

ARIADNE
Poor Theseus! Your bravery and sword
Will not exempt you from the horrid fate
That doth await you in my father's maze:
The Labyrinth of Minos, King of Crete,
From which no man hath e'er emerged alive.
'Twas made so cunningly, with passages
That, like the serpent, wind upon themselves,
That Daedalus, my father's architect,
Upon completion of the edifice,
Could hardly find the way to save himself.
For many weary years, my charge hath been
To tend my father's merciless device,
Wherein I have beheld unnumbered men

Perish within its cruel passageways;
For if you slay the monster, Minotaur,
Half man, half bull, whom no man hath defeated,
You'll wither ere you find the proper path
That leads you from these walls to liberty.
And yet, of all the wretched men that sought
To triumph o'er my father's savage maze,
Thou art the first whom I desire to see
Emerge from forth these walls unharmed, alive.
And therefore, daring Theseus of Athens,
I shall defy my father's strict commands
And teach thee how to overcome, with ease,
The monstrous death that lies behind these gates;
In recompense whereof, I shall require
This earnest gesture of thy gratitude:
That when your ships depart the isle of Crete,
I shall accompany you back to Athens,
Where you shall take me as thy loving wife;
For thou hast killed the monster of my pride,
Brave Theseus, and found the hidden pathway
That leadeth to my heart. How say you then?
I'll save your life, if you will marry me,
If not, my love shall perish here with thee.

Exit ARIADNE.

JOHN
What's the next one?

HENRY
It's Calpurnia.

[PROJECTION: The Palace of Julius Caesar, Rome]

JOHN
Calpurnia...?

HENRY
Julius Caesar's wife?

JOHN
Oh, yes...

HENRY
One of the speeches that William cut.

JOHN
Which speech?

HENRY
Her sage advice to her husband...?

JOHN
About...?

HENRY
About refusing the crown in public...

CALPURNIA
How now, my love? What business, lord, so early?
Art headed to the feast of Lupercal?
'Tis rumored they intend to offer you
A kingly coronet; that Antony,
Before the common citizens of Rome
That traffic in the open marketplace,
Will offer you the emperorship of Rome.
But hear, my husband, hear, my Julius:
You must not seek to wear a royal crown.
When they do offer it, you must refuse,
Yea, put it by, with fair humility,
And let the Roman people clearly see
You do not seek the yoke of sovereignty,
But rather, hope to be a faithful servant

To the Republic, as great Pompey was,
Not driven by a clambering ambition,
By vanity, self-love, or arrogance.
For present times are perilous, good Caesar,
No time to be proclaimed an emperor,
For that our stony-hearted enemies,
The privileged patricians of the Senate,
Do fear thee as an over-mounting threat,
And shall do all they can to hinder thee
From seizing on a power absolute,
Even to the point of bloody butchery.
Dismiss me not for that I am a woman
Who nothing knows of matters politic,
But pray you, husband, mark my counsel well;
For heaven knows, my father was a consul,
My brother is a consul, and indeed,
Had I been born a man, I would myself
A consul of the Roman senate be!
Therefore, refuse to don the crown, my love;
For, though I am a woman and thy wife,
'Tis wisdom that, observed, may save thy life.

Exit CALPURNIA.

HENRY
Ah, I remember this one!

JOHN
Which?

HENRY
That Audrey speech?

JOHN
Hmm...

HENRY
The shepherd girl from *As You Like It*?

[PROJECTION: The Forest of Arden]

(We hear birds chirping softly in the trees.)

JOHN
Yes...?

HENRY
Breaking up with William...?

JOHN
Oh, yes. Why did he cut that?

HENRY
You know...to punish that actor...

JOHN
The boy playing Audrey?

HENRY
That's right.

JOHN
Ouch!

(JOHN, who is seated, becomes William.)

AUDREY
God ye good morrow, William. I am glad to see you, for I
desire a word with you, if you be at leisure. We have been good
neighbors, William, since we were barnes, have we not? Good
friends? As children, we did play together, and work together,
and share in all. You have milked my cows, and I have slept in

your hayloft. You have plowed my fields and I have pulled your radishes. You have fished my brook, and I have scattered your seed. So you know that I am fond of you, William. Very fond. And yet—I know not how to tell you—I do love another. For, much against my will, the gentleman that came here from the court hath won my heart. Dost know the man I mean? He that will woo in rhyme, and cut a caper, and finger the pipe, and speak in long sentences, and make merry every waking hour of the day? Hast heard he doth desire to marry me? 'Tis true—he asked me to be his wife, and I could not say nay, for I do laugh when I am in his company—though I know not why I laugh, for much of what he says I do not understand. And yet, I hope that you will understand me now, good William. And that we will still be good friends. Good neighbors. And that my goats may still graze in your good pasture. What say you, William? William?

Exit AUDREY.

HENRY
Here's a good one!

JOHN
Who's that?

HENRY
It's Hero.

JOHN
Hero from *Much Ado*...?

HENRY
No, Hero from *Hero and Leander.*

[PROJECTION: A Tower in Sestos, Overlooking the Hellespont]

JOHN
Leander? Who's Leander?

HENRY
Remember? Hero's lover.

JOHN
Hmmm...

HENRY
Hero lives in a tower on one side of the Hellespont, in Sestos...

JOHN
Yes...

HENRY
And Leander, her lover, lives on the other side of the channel, in Abydos...

JOHN
Ah...

(We hear a storm at sea, and occasional thunder.)

HENRY
So he has to swim across the strait to see her every night...

JOHN
And swim back across to get home again?

HENRY
You got it.

(HENRY goes to his knees to become Leander, who gazes intently at the channel below.)

HERO

I prithee, go not yet, gentle Leander!
Do not attempt to swim across the strait,
My love, to thine own dwelling in Abydos!
For look, the night is dark as any tomb,
The timid moon conceals her ashen face,
And our familiar stars are smothered 'neath
A melancholy shroud. Summer is gone,
And now the Hellespont runs swift and high,
The savage winds do whip the frantic sea
And pelt these groaning casements with salt tears.
No going forth tonight, my dearest love!
O stay with me within these stony walls,
Atop the tower that scorns these mighty gales
And shuns the ebbing surges of the flood,
For these two arms are surely warmer, love,
Than the embracement of the icy sea.
Then, kiss me, love; come, drench me in thy kisses,
And do not stop until the storm be passed,
For I do fear that every kiss shall be
The final taste of summer's ecstasy.
Tomorrow, when the sun doth rise, my love,
The channel once again will be serene,
Like lovers drowsing in a morning bed,
Why, then you may descend these marble steps,
And let the current take thy manly frame
Into her arms, as gentle as mine own.
But for tonight, Leander, for tonight,
I do beseech, plunge not thy naked body
Into the black and spiteful Hellespont
Where, if you were to perish in the sea,
My soul must chase thee to eternity!

(HERO takes Leander's hands and leads him gently towards an exit...)

Exit HERO.

JOHN
What's next?

HENRY
It's Nell, the kitchen wench.

[PROJECTION: The Kitchen in Antipholus' House in
Ephesus]

JOHN
The kitchen wench? Really?

HENRY
From *The Comedy of Errors*.

JOHN
I vaguely remember...

(We hear kitchen sounds—boiling water and chopping.)

HENRY
She's in love with Dromio of Ephesus...

JOHN
Yes...

HENRY
But ends up chasing Dromio of Syracuse by mistake...

JOHN
His twin brother...?

HENRY
Exactly!

(JOHN becomes Dromio of Syracuse, sitting at the base of the stove, while HENRY sits on the other side, mirroring him.)

NELL
(Stirring a mixing bowl with a spoon)
O for shame, Dromio! Is it not enough? Is it not enough that I must sweat in this hot kitchen every day, feeding this fiery stove from morn to night, enduring the curses of master Antipholus, the blows of Adriana, the gossip of the servants, but that you must mock me, too? Pretend not to know me? Out upon thee, naughty varlet! You know me well enough when thy greedy maw doth draw thee to my table. You know me well enough when there's a sausage to be served; you know me well enough when there's a sugared bowl to lick; you know me well enough when there's muffins to be had, or tenderloin to sample, or rump roast to devour! Yea, thou hast a stomach for me then! Then are thy famished fingers everywhere! Then do I behold thy nose in my pies, thy lips in my sauces, thy tongue in my custards! But when thy lusty appetites are sated, how dost thou thank me? By spurning me? By furrowing thy brow and running off without bestowing me a kiss! Alack, that I was born to dote on such a man as thee! 'Tis a blessing two such men can never tread the earth at once, for then should all the world run mad!

Exit NELL.

(JOHN rises, in distress.)

JOHN
Can we take a little break?

HENRY
A break?

JOHN
You know. To...

HENRY
Oh!

JOHN
Just a quick one.

HENRY
Well...sure, okay.

JOHN
Ten minutes, tops.

HENRY
Okay.

(JOHN begins to exit; HENRY stops him abruptly.)

Wait! I'll come, too.

JOHN
Okay.

(Offstage, we hear a door open as both JOHN and HENRY exit.)

HENRY
And no napping now!

JOHN
Of course not!

(We hear the door close; the candles continue to burn, as the lights fade.)

End of Act One

INTERMISSION

ACT TWO

(JOHN and HENRY enter, first one then the other, zipping up their flies.)

HENRY
Feel better?

JOHN
Definitely.

HENRY
Good! Time for a drink?

JOHN
No, let's look at some more.

HENRY
Tomorrow.

JOHN
More!

HENRY
Tomorrow.

JOHN
More, I prithee, more!

HENRY
Alright, okay.

JOHN
What's this one?

HENRY
It's Margaret.

JOHN
Queen Margaret from *Henry the Sixth?*

HENRY
No...this is Margaret from *Much Ado About Nothing*.

[PROJECTION: Governor Leonato's House, Messina]

JOHN
There's a Margaret in *Much Ado*...?

HENRY
Remember? The waiting gentlewoman to Hero?

JOHN
Okay...

HENRY
Who dresses up in Hero's clothes...?

JOHN
The one who meets her beau at Hero's window after dark...?

HENRY
That's right! Borachio...

JOHN
Which is seen by Claudio...

HENRY
Hero's fiancé...

JOHN
Who thinks she's sleeping around...

HENRY
And casts her off at their wedding the next day!

JOHN
Right, so Margaret figures out the plot before anyone else
does...

HENRY
Exactly...

MARGARET
Ay me, can this be so? I am ashamed
To think it! O my gentle mistress Hero,
Dishonored and disgraced at her own wedding
By Signor Claudio and by Don Pedro!
Shamed publicly upon the very altar
Where her betrothèd should have married her!
Alack, alack the day! What have I done?
'Twas I that spoke covertly with a man
At Hero's open window yesternight!
For, yielding to Borachio's entreaties,
I dressed myself in Hero's night attire,
And, as the bells of midnight sweetly chimed
From forth the tower of the holy chapel,
I spoke with him from out the open casement
Of Hero's chambers, as he had appointed.
I must confess my scandalous transgression!
Yet, how can I divulge my great offense?
I'll lose my place if this affair be known!
How now, shall I be mute and tender not

A strong defense of the defenseless Hero?
Borachio, thou ignominious villain!
To use me as a lure in this vile plot
To stain the reputation of a maiden?
Don John, no doubt hath put him to this deed.
I'll find the man and force him to confess;
The wrongs against this maid must have redress.

Exit MARGARET.

JOHN
What's that one?

HENRY
It's from *The Jew of Venice*.

[PROJECTION: The Venetian Ghetto]

JOHN
Ah—the play about young Shylock?

HENRY
Yes.

JOHN
And who is that?

HENRY
It's Leah.

JOHN
Shylock's wife?

HENRY
Yes, as a young woman.

JOHN
Ah.

HENRY
Shylock just proposed marriage to her, but...

JOHN
But?

HENRY
She has one condition...

(HENRY sits down to become Shelach.)

LEAH
Yet one thing more, dear Shelach, you must do
Before I may consent to be your wife.
This ring belonged to my belovèd father,
To Yitzhak, may his memory be a blessing.
For fifty years, it never left his finger,
Gracing his daily labors with the stone,
A flawless turquoise by Egyptians found
Beneath the deserts of the holy land.
This precious gift was given to him by
My father's father, Avram, peace be with him,
Who three rings indistinguishable made
From that Egyptian turquoise, fashioning
A matching gem for each of his three sons,
That each would know his equal love for them
And quarrel not, as brothers often will.
My father gave this treasured ring to me
The day before he died, entrusting me,
By solemn vow, before I came to wed,
To place it on the hand of my betroth'd
To bind his soul entirely to my love.
To you, Shelach, I give this family treasure,

As I do give the treasure of my heart,
And do entreat you now, in sight of God,
In honor of my father's memory,
To wear it on thy finger till thy death,
And never be so careless as to lose it.
Do this for me, and I shall be thy wife
And make a home for our new family.
May God in heaven bless our sacred union
With happiness, with health, with perfect joy,
And most of all, with many precious children!

(LEAH takes Shelach's hand, walking quietly with him toward an exit...)

Exit LEAH.

HENRY
I'm sure you'll remember this.

JOHN
Yes?

HENRY
This is young Cleopatra.

[PROJECTION: The Villa of Julius Caesar in Rome]

JOHN
From *Antony and Cleopatra?*

HENRY
No, from *Caesar and Cleopatra.*

JOHN
Of course...

HENRY
The morning of Caesar's assassination.

JOHN
Yes...

(In the distance, we hear havoc in the streets.)

HENRY
She's been living in Rome in one of Caesar's villas...

JOHN
With their young son, Caesarion, yes?...

HENRY
Yes...

JOHN
And she figures she'll be next?

HENRY
Exactly.

CLEOPATRA
O Charmian, hast heard the news? He's dead!
Struck down by his most trusted countrymen
As he did make his way unto the Senate.
Great Caesar, dead. Alack, his lifeless body
Still lies a-bleeding there, in purpled robes,
Staining the pristine stones of Pompey's Porch.
Confusion now doth reign in Roman streets,
And havoc is afoot throughout the city.
Alack, who shall be next to fall and die?
Shall Caesar's kindred and his loyal friends
Be subject to this savage butchery?
Mark Antony must surely think it so,

For rumor's flighty tongue doth whisper forth
That he hath fled the city in disguise.
Alas, good Charmian, I fear now for
The safety of our house, for all our lives,
And for the life of my young son, Caesarion,
For that mine enemies in bleeding Rome,
Incensed by the pernicious Cicero,
Despise me for my influence with Caesar,
Reviling me amongst the senators
For swelling still his sovereignly ambition,
His appetite for diadems of gold.
Quick, Charmian, order the wagons loaded,
For I shall leave this fearful place tonight.
The crooked road down the Janiculum,
Shall lead us secretly to Tiber banks,
Where we shall trace the river to the coast,
Then southward ride to reach the port of Naples.
Once there, we'll hoist our alabaster sails,
And, hazarding Messina's narrow straits,
Make way to sunlit Alexandria.
I prithee, make all speedy haste for home,
For I shall ne'er set foot again in Rome.

Exit CLEOPATRA.

JOHN
Okay, what's next?

HENRY
Kate Keepdown.

[PROJECTION: In the Streets of Vienna]

JOHN
Ah, from *The Taming of the Shrew?*

HENRY
No that's a different Kate.

JOHN
Oh, Kate! The French Princess at the end of *Henry the Fifth*.

HENRY
No, that's a different Kate.

JOHN
Oh, Kate, Hotspur's wife.

HENRY
No, that's different Kate.

JOHN
Oh, Kate, Henry the Eighth's first wife.

HENRY
No, that's a different Kate.

JOHN
Okay, then who? Kate who...?

HENRY
Kate Keepdown...

JOHN
Right, who the devil is Kate Keepdown?

HENRY
She's a young maiden, Lucio's lover in *Measure for Measure*...

JOHN
Lucio...he's the rakish gentleman?

HENRY
That's the one. He got Kate Keepdown pregnant and then
abandons her...

JOHN
Which comes back to bite him in the end...?

HENRY
Oh, yes...

KATE KEEPDOWN
What, Lucio! Will you conceal your face
And turn your back upon me? O, for shame!
Nay, villain, do not walk away from me!
How now? Wilt thou pretend thou dost not know me?
O villainous dissembler! I am Kate,
Brought up to be a lady in the best
Of Viennese society; that Kate
To whom you did profess your lasting love,
And made a vow to take in holy wedlock;
That Kate who, at thy urging, left her home
And family to give herself to thee;
That Kate whom thou didst bring into thy bed
To fill her virgin belly up with child;
That Kate, whom thou didst cruelly abandon,
Condemning her to roam Vienna's streets
To seek a place of shelter and of solace.
Thy son, alack the day, was swaddled in
The filthy linens of a bawdy-house,
Where he did weep and wail throughout the night
That he was born to such a heinous father.
If not for Mistress Overdone, Sir Knave,
Who made a place for us beneath her roof,
We would be sleeping in Vienna streets,
And surely would have starved to death by this.

To her I am beholden for my life,
And sell my body now to pay our debts.
O, Lucio! Wilt thou not make us whole?
I know thou hast no tenderness for me,
But will you not provide for your own son?
You must not now deny the boy is thine:
In flesh and blood he is thy very copy!
Therefore, I say, thou shalt do right by us,
Or I shall tell the Provost of these crimes,
And cry out 'justice!' till my pleas be heard.
Though I to prison may be sent as well,
Right glad I'll be to join thee in a cell!

Exit KATE KEEPDOWN.

HENRY
I remember this one...

JOHN
What have you got there?

HENRY
It's from *Venus and Adonis*.

[PROJECTION: A Clearing in the Woods]

JOHN
The poem?

HENRY
No...remember? He tried to write it as a play?

JOHN
Oh, right.

HENRY
So this is Venus, in a clearing in the woods, trying to seduce the handsome young hunter...

(We hear the gentle, mesmerizing vibrato of bells.)

JOHN
That's Adonis?

HENRY
That's right, but he's very young, and he'd rather go hunting...

VENUS
Vouchsafe, Adonis, to alight thy steed,
And rein his proud head to the saddle-bow;
If thou wilt deign this favor, for thy meed
A thousand honey secrets shalt thou know:
Here come and sit, where never serpent hisses,
And being set, I'll smother thee with kisses.
Touch but my lips with those fair lips of thine—
Though mine be not so fair, yet are they red—
The kiss shall be thine own as well as mine.
What seest thou in the ground? hold up thy head:
Look in mine eye-balls, there thy beauty lies;
Then why not lips on lips, since eyes in eyes?
Art thou ashamed to kiss? then wink again,
And I will wink; so shall the day seem night.
Love keeps his revels where there are but twain;
Be bold to play, our sport is not in sight.
These blue-vein'd violets whereon we lean
Never can blab, nor know not what we mean.
O gentle boy, since I have hemm'd thee here
Within the circuit of this ivory pale,
I'll be a park, and thou shalt be my deer:
Feed where thou wilt, on mountain or in dale;

Graze on my lips; and if those hills be dry,
Stray lower, where the pleasant fountains lie.
Within this limit is relief enough,
Sweet bottom-grass and high delightful plain,
Round rising hillocks, brakes obscure and rough,
To shelter thee from tempest and from rain:
Then be my deer, since I am such a park;
No dog shall rouse thee, though a thousand bark.
O, pity Venus, thou flint-hearted boy!
'Tis but a kiss I beg; why art thou coy?

(VENUS follows Adonis into the woods...)

Exit VENUS.

JOHN
Who's that?

HENRY
Ophelia.

[PROJECTION: Ophelia's Bedchamber, the Castle at Elsinore]

JOHN
Hamlet's girlfriend?

HENRY
Yes.

JOHN
William cut one of her speeches?

HENRY
Well, you know...the play was long!

JOHN
So long! Like crazy long! Which speech?

HENRY
After the nunnery scene.

JOHN
Oh! Where she reveals...?

HENRY
Exactly...

OPHELIA
A nunnery? Alack, my dearest Hamlet!
What holy place shall shelter me, while this,
Our flower of love, doth blossom in my womb?
O growing consequence of rash impatience,
Where shall we go? What shall we do? How live?
For when we are discover'd in the court,
My father shall deny that I was born,
My brother disavow me as his blood,
The King and Queen shall curse my very name
And banish you and I from their dominions.
And wilt thou, loving Hamlet, stand aloof
As I am driven out of paradise,
Ophelia, who should have been thy wife,
To lands unknown, and accents never heard,
To live upon the charity of strangers?
O holy Mary, how shall I prevent this?
Some remedy to salve these mortal wounds!
I've read in books the bitter leaves of rue,
Consumed in superfluity, can stop
The vital pulse within a woman's womb,
So fatal is it to a life unborn.
And now I do bethink me, such an herb
Doth grow in Gertrude's garden. There I'll go,
To pluck the potent herb that shall undo

The burden of my budding motherhood.
And yet, I fear I shall forever rue
The very thing that I set out to do.
For, by my Christendom, what might I be
Had mine own mother done as much to me!

Exit OPHELIA.

HENRY
Ready for this?

JOHN
Hit me, baby.

HENRY
It's Nemesis.

[PROJECTION: A Reflecting Pool in the Forest]

JOHN
Nemesis?

HENRY
The goddess of divine retribution?

JOHN
Huh...

HENRY
From *Echo and Narcissus*.

JOHN
Don't remember that one.

HENRY
Sure you do.

JOHN
Drawing a blank here.

HENRY
The young hunter Narcissus spurns the love of Echo...

JOHN
Echo?

HENRY
Echo. The mountain nymph...

JOHN
The mountain nymph?

HENRY
Yes, the mountain nymph.

JOHN
Huh.

HENRY
So...the goddess Nemesis devises a way to punish him...

(HENRY falls under the spell of NEMESIS, stooping upon command.)

NEMESIS
What seest thou, young Narcissus, in the pool?
Yea, stoop, and view what is reflected there.
Such beauty, such magnificence, such grace!
Alas, those radiant eyes, that silken hair,
Those crimson lips, that rugged chin, that smile:
The pinnacle of nature's handiwork!
Hast ever seen the like? How now, brave hunter?
Canst thou not speak? Nor move? Nor break this gaze?
O proud Narcissus, arrogant young man,

As impudent as thou art beautiful,
Thy high renown has reached mine ears,
Along with word of thy disdainful deeds!
Didst thou not spurn the gentle wood-nymph, Echo,
Who, smitten with thy beauty and thy grace,
Did follow thee into the forest, where,
O shameful man, thou didst with scorn abuse her?
Thy cruelty did break her tender heart,
And now she hides herself in distant glens,
In yawning valleys and in steep ravines,
Her muted, murmured, mirror-like replies
The only affirmation of her presence.
'Tis for her sake I come to censure thee,
By luring thee to view this glassy pool;
For I am Nemesis, goddess of Justice,
Stern punisher of pride and insolence,
Who doles out suffering and loss to those
Who do forget the bounty of their blessings.
Then languish here upon thy knees, young man,
Held captive in this miserable rapture
Wherein thy love can never be requited;
And when thy deep despair becomes too great,
Then slip beneath the surface of the pool,
And drown thyself in love, thou doting fool!

Exit NEMESIS.

JOHN
And this is...?

(JOHN drops HENRY's portfolio on the floor in front of him, breaking the spell.)

HENRY
Oh! It's Nell.

JOHN
From The Comedy of Errors?

HENRY
No, from *Falstaff in Love*.

[PROJECTION: The Boarshead Tavern, Eastcheap, London]

JOHN
Oh, yes—the play he tried to write for Queen Elizabeth....

HENRY
Except he couldn't finish it...

JOHN
So he wrote *Merry Wives of Windsor* instead!

(HENRY grimaces in disdain.)

HENRY
Yes. So this is Nell, the young daughter of the Host of the Boarshead Inn...

JOHN
In Eastcheap?

HENRY
Right, in Eastcheap, where Falstaff spends all his time...

JOHN
And his money.

(We hear Falstaff snoring offstage.)

HENRY
Right. So this is a young Nell in the tavern, dreaming of a
better life...

NELL
I have left Sir John a-sleeping in my bed. I had much to do to
put him down last night, for he's a man of ravenous appetites.
Three times he spent himself before he fell asleep. Each time
he cried out "Mary!" Is he so religious? Alas, despite myself, I
cannot help be fond of him. Too fond, i' faith, for he can never
care for such a one as I. Why, he is dubbed a royal knight, and I
a tapster's daughter. He serves the King, and I serve scoundrels.
He rides a-horseback, and I ride customers. I know he cannot
love me, yet, alas, my heart cannot but dote on him. O to be
the wife of a knight! To leave my father, to leave this tavern, to
leave the company of men who treat me worse than common
dirt. There is example for it: John of Gaunt married his child's
nursemaid and made her Lady Katherine, Duchess of Lancaster.
Why should not I be Lady Falstaff, Duchess of Eastcheap?
Then should I have eight servants to wait upon me, saying yes,
m'lady, no, m'lady, anon, m'lady, running to fetch and scrape and
pour, whilst I, sitting upon a velvet couch, dressed in silk and
gold, play with my pearl and contemplate the tapestries, having
come from my chambers, where I have left a satisfied Sir John
asleep. Ah, what sweetness! What bliss!

Exit NELL.

HENRY
Had enough?

JOHN
Not yet—another!

HENRY
This one's from *The Life of Fulvia of Rome.*

[PROJECTION: The Home of Antony and Fulvia, Rome]

JOHN
And Fulvia is...?

HENRY
Mark Antony's wife.

JOHN
Ah.

HENRY
They were, like, a Roman power couple...?

JOHN
Ah yes, of course...I knew that.

HENRY
So when Antony decides to stay in Egypt with Cleopatra...

JOHN
She's not a happy camper!

(FULVIA snatches the letter from HENRY and reads.)

FULVIA
O lech'rous villain! Not return from Egypt?
Will Antony, with his Egyptian whore,
Remain in Alexandria? And what
Shall I do here in Rome? Wait patiently
For his return like an obedient wife?
Remain at home and spin upon a wheel?
I, Fulvia, who did defend great Rome
While Antony and bold Octavius
Gave chase to Marcus Brutus and his band
Of bloody-minded traitors 'round the globe?

I, who commanded all affairs of state
And held the vasty empire in my hands
While Antony did couch in luxury
Upon a truant bed of silk and gold!
I, who curtailed the doltish Lepidus,
Third pillar of the universal world,
And taught him how to come when I do call?
I, who impaled the cold and lifeless tongue
Of spiteful Cicero with golden hairpins
To stay that nimble instrument of malice
From railing on us from the world beyond?
I, who imposed my will upon the Senate,
Knowing the way to forge alliances,
To auction provinces, and levy fines,
To bribe, to cheat, abuse, extort, obstruct,
And favor friends as well as any man?
And shall I sit upon a stool and watch
The world go 'round? No! Fulvia
Will not an idle housewife be! Not while
Our enemies do gather on all sides
With deep designs to bring us to our knees!
No, Antony, if thou no interest hast
In thy affairs and fortunes here at home,
I must and shall take action in thy stead.
I'll join with Lucius, Antony's young brother,
To fight against Octavius in Rome.
Eight legions Lucius hath at his command:
Sufficient men to occupy the city.
If Antony will not defend his realm,
Then I shall take up arms, and wear his helm!

Exit FULVIA.

JOHN
And this is...?

HENRY
Jessica.

JOHN
Ah, Jessica!...Jessica who?

HENRY
Shylock's daughter?

JOHN
Yes, from *The Merchant of Venice.*

HENRY
No, this is from *The Jew of Venice.* Remember?

[PROJECTION: The Jewish Cemetery, Venice]

JOHN
Oh right, the play about Shylock.

HENRY
Right.

JOHN
So...?

HENRY
So, it's been a year since Shylock's wife died...

JOHN
Shylock's wife is...?

HENRY
Leah?

JOHN
Yes, Leah, I remember...

HENRY
So, here, Jessica visits her mother's grave to seek her advice...

(We hear wind blowing coldly through the graveyard.)

(JESSICA kisses a small stone and places it on her mother's grave.)

JESSICA
Look down, dear mother, look upon the earth
And hear the lamentations of thy daughter,
Thy Jessica, who on this solemn day,
The annual remembrance of thy death,
Unto thy everlasting bed hath come
To say a prayer to thy departed spirit.
O mother, who endured to give me life,
Who fed me and protected me from harm
From my first breath until thy very last,
Whose boundless love still beats within my heart,
I prithee, counsel me from thy celestial seat,
For lo, I must confess, I am in love.
Lorenzo is the young Venetian's name,
A handsome gentleman who took my part
Upon the steps of the Rialto Bridge.
He says he wants to marry me, dear mother,
And yet, I know not how to answer him,
For that—I fear it shall distress you much
To learn—he lives not in the Ghetto Nuovo
Among the people of our covenant.
He is a Gentile, mother, not a Jew.
He asks me now to cast away my faith,
To be his wife, and to become a Christian.
I dare not broach this business with my father,
For he hath altered much since you did leave us:

Questioning God for taking his dear wife,
Pronouncing curses on his enemies,
And locking up our doors against the world.
And though I dearly love and honor him,
As any daughter should revere her father,
I cannot help be fearful of him, too.
O mother, counsel me. What shall I do?

Exit JESSICA.

HENRY
Oh, I forgot about this...

JOHN
Who's this?

HENRY
This is Emilia.

JOHN
Right! Iago's wife from *Othello*.

HENRY
No, she's from *Winter's Tale*.

[PROJECTION: The Royal Court of King Leontes, Sicilia]

JOHN
That doesn't ring a bell.

HENRY
Queen Hermione's Lady-in-Waiting?

JOHN
Sorry, I got nothing.

HENRY
Remember, Hermione is imprisoned by King Leontes, her
jealous husband?

JOHN
Okay...

HENRY
And then her young son Mamillius dies of grief?

JOHN
Yes...

HENRY
So Emilia's the lady who sends word to the court that Mamillius
is dead.

(HENRY hands EMILIA a child's stuffed toy—a small lion.)

EMILIA
What? Is he dead? Is our belovèd prince
Deceased? O poor Mamillius! Alack,
My heart shall split in twain! How can this be?
Is't possible a child may die of grief?
Yea, now I do perceive that deep despair
May fatal prove to one so pure of heart.
Hermione, I fear now for thy life,
For this shall kill thee, gracious queen, outright!
Is't not enough, you gods, our lady must endure
The trial of her honesty, adjudged
By lily-liver'd lords who lack the gall
To stand upon the honor of their Queen
Against the ravings of a lunatic,
But now she must withstand the heavy loss
Of her belovèd son? For shame, Leontes!
King of cruelty! Thou dost deserve to live

In infamy for this sweet child's death.
Search every corner of the vasty globe,
No absolution shalt thou find among
The most forgiving souls upon the earth.
Mamillius, dear boy, I must believe
The gods have ta'en thee from thy mother's arms,
To spare thee from thy father's tyrannies.
In that distressful thought I must find comfort.
Go thou, deliver these ill tidings to the court.
Break off proceedings, and inform the King
His son hath ceased all earthly suffering.

Exit EMILIA.

JOHN
And who is this?

HENRY
This is Dorcas.

[PROJECTION: A Sheep Sheering Festival in Bohemia]

JOHN
Dorcas?...From?

HENRY
She's one of the two shepherdesses from *The Winter's Tale.*

JOHN
Oh, from Bohemia!

HENRY
Right.

(In the distance, we hear the bleating of sheep.)

JOHN
And the other is Mopsa, right?

HENRY
Right. And they're old friends...

JOHN
Yes, but they're in love with the same young man...

HENRY
Yes, a clownish young shepherd...

DORCAS
Look at him fawn upon Mopsa, buying her ribbons and gloves
and sweetmeats at this our sheep-sheering! See how she hangs
on him, holding him by the arm and doting on his every word!
How she kisses his cheek with her stinking garlic breath.
O to be misused by my best friend like this! Nay, she is
practically a sister! For we came into this world like twins, born
at an instant, and instantly inseparable. Our mothers did rock
us in one cradle, swaddle us in one blanket, feed us from one
bosom, shelter us under one roof. And to be betrayed like this
by a sister, it goes hard! What a fool I was to lie down with
him in the hayloft! To let him sample that which he should
purchase. Why did I ever lie down with him? I thought he
loved me. For he did swear upon the heavens that he did.
O lying slave! Now is he enthralled with Mopsa, sparing no
expense to buy her every little gift her heart desires. He hopes
to win her maidenhood, too! O men! Why must they desire
most the thing they cannot have? And yet, why should I desire
such a one as this? Alack, I cannot help myself! The heart wants
what it wants. And my broken heart doth pine for him. For
that he's funny. And handsome. And large. Hearted. Alack, how
shall I win him back again? I'll put myself between these doves,
and win his heart once more. For I can smile more brightly,

and sing more sweetly, and dance more lightly, and speak more charmingly, and laugh more endearingly than any thieving sister in Bohemia!

Exit DORCAS.

HENRY
Oh, boy...

JOHN
What?

HENRY
Ha.

JOHN
What??

HENRY
It's Rosaline.

JOHN
From *Love's Labor's Lost?*

HENRY
No.

JOHN
No?

HENRY
From *Love's Labor's Won.*

[PROJECTION: The Royal Palace, Paris]

JOHN
The sequel?

HENRY
Yes...remember?

JOHN
Of course I do...I just...gimme a hint...

HENRY
At the end of *Love's Labor's Lost*, the death of the King of France
starts a European war...

JOHN
Yes...

HENRY
So four years later, at the signing of an armistice in Paris, all the
lovers are poised to reunite...

JOHN
Got it...

HENRY
But Rosaline has been disguised as a journalist during the war...

JOHN
Uh-huh...

HENRY
When she gets a letter from the Princess...

ROSALINE
(Reading a letter)
"My dearest Rosaline, I crave thy counsel

And sage advice on grave affairs of state;
Return, therefore, with all convenient speed,
To Paris, where the crownèd heads of Europe
Do congregate to árbitrate a treaty."
Obeying thus the will of my dear Princess,
I dutifully have returned to Paris;
But yet I do remain in this disguise,
A correspondent armed with ink and pen,
Wherein I boldly counterfeit a man,
For in it, I have seen with mine own eyes
The field of battle; heard with mine own ears
The sound of skirmish, smelled with mine own nose
The stench of death, and with these faculties,
Made sharp upon the whetstone of this war,
I hope to witness these hostilities
Protracted in a gentlemanly fashion,
Exchanging smoke-filled rooms for smoke-filled skies,
Dull statesmanship for lethal marksmanship,
Long tables for deep trenches, tired phrases
For tired forces, folded arms for loaded arms,
And write all down to share with all the world.
I'll stay, therefore, a man, until that time
When war's death knells, and bells of peace do chime.
But who is he comes here? It is Berowne!

Exit ROSALINE.

JOHN
What have you got next?

HENRY
Lady Jane Grey.

[PROJECTION: The Tower Green, The Tower of London, 1554]

JOHN
The one who was Queen of England for, like, a week?

HENRY
Yes, she was a Protestant...

JOHN
Right, but then she was imprisoned...

HENRY
In the Tower of London...

JOHN
For high treason...

HENRY
By Henry the Eighth's oldest daughter...

JOHN
Queen Mary...

HENRY
A Catholic...

JOHN
Who sentenced Jane to death...

HENRY
Upon the Tower green...

(JOHN and HENRY march upstage in unison and turn to become guards.)

(We hear a crowd murmuring.)

LADY JANE GREY
Good people, I am hither come to die,
For by a law, the Council hath proclaimed
I am a faithless traitor to the crown.
The acts, indeed, against Queen Mary's highness,
I do acknowledge freely were unlawful,
And the consenting thereunto by me:
But touching the desire and procurement
Of England's royal throne, by me, or by
My friends on my behalf, before my God,
I wash my hands thereof in innocency,
For I did never wish to be a queen,
Nor never sought the way to wear a crown,
Nor never hoped to sit upon a throne.
Before my God, and all of you assembled,
I pray you bear me witness that today
I die a true and faithful Christian woman,
And that I look this morning to be saved
By no means other than the mercy of my God
And by the merits of his only son,
Who shed his blood to cleanse us of our sins.
I do confess, though I did know the word of God,
I did neglect the same and loved myself,
And therefore is this plague or punishment
Most happily befallen unto me
For all the evil I have done before His eyes.
Yet, I thank God most humbly for His goodness
That he hath given me sufficient time
And respite to repent my grievous sins.
Therefore, good people, while I am alive,
I pray you to assist me with your prayers.
Into thy hands, O Lord, my spirit I commend.
I pray you, gentleman, dispatch me quickly.

(She closes her eyes. We hear an axe falling violently, as the stage turns red.)

Exit LADY JANE GREY.

HENRY
Time for a drink?

JOHN
Just a few more. Who's that?

HENRY
It's Rosaline.

JOHN
Ah, from *Love's Labor's Lost.*

HENRY
No.

JOHN
Oh, from *Love's Labor's Won.*

HENRY
No, from *Romeo and Rosaline.*

[PROJECTION: The Villa of the Capulets, Verona]

JOHN
I don't think so...that can't be.

HENRY
Yes, she's Romeo's first crush...remember?

JOHN
Absolutely not.

HENRY
Sure you do. Romeo is in love with Rosaline before he meets
Juliet at the Capulet party?

JOHN
Oh, yes! Rosaline! He's heartsick over her...

HENRY
Right! So this was an early draft...

JOHN
When Romeo's courting her?

HENRY
Yes...

JOHN
And he's getting nowhere fast...

HENRY
Exactly.

(ROSALINE *takes the letter from* HENRY, *who becomes Mercutio.*)

ROSALINE
What's this? Ay me! Too well I know the hand.
Another missive from that Montague?
Go to, Mercutio! Mock not my grief,
Rude man, for this great flood of sugared words,
These silken phrases and these tortured rhymes
That tender his devotion unto death,
Nay, from the grave, are most intolerable!
He is a friend of yours, this Romeo,
Is it not so? Nay, do not now deny it,
For I have seen thee in Verona's streets
Carousing with this spaniel and his pack

Of filthy Montagues. For shame, Mercutio,
To proffer me the missives of a fool!
Ay, he's a fool, good sir, a doting fool,
With no more manly virtue than a flea.
Why, we have not exchanged a dozen words
Yet he presumes we are betroth'd, our names
Set down in heaven's book as man and wife!
Nay, his epistles hear, and be you judge:
"O sweetest Rosaline, the all-seeing sun
Ne'er saw thy match since first the world begun."
Lord, what a fawning puppy! Mark what follows:
"Do not forswear to love, for in that vow
I shall live dead that live to tell it now."
Alack, I cannot overlook the rest!
Are there no sonnets from your gallant cousin,
The county Paris? Marry, such a man!
This Romeo is but a toad to him,
A sheep, a boar, an ass, a gaping pig!
In sooth, I shall not answer his appeals,
For that will spurn his pen to set down more;
But when thou see'st him in Verona's streets,
Mercutio, say this: I cannot now,
Nor never shall, consent to be his love,
And when the morning comes that I shall wed,
If Montague, then they shall find me dead.
Go tell him so, and bring me no more verse!

Exit ROSALINE.

JOHN
Who's next?

HENRY
This is Lucrece.

[PROJECTION: The Home of General Collatine, Rome]

JOHN
From *The Rape of Lucrece?*

HENRY
Yes—but the play, not the poem.

JOHN
There was a play?

HENRY
Unfinished.

JOHN
Didn't know that...

HENRY
So Lucrece is the wife of a Roman general...

JOHN
Yes, I remember, Collatine...

HENRY
And she's raped in her own bedroom by an honored guest...

JOHN
By Tarquin, the King's of Rome's son...

HENRY
Right...so this is the next morning...

(JOHN and HENRY stand to either side of the stage as two lords.)

LUCRECE
Dear husband Collatine, and you fair lords,
My poor laments would be drawn out too long
To tell them all with one poor tired tongue.

Then be this all the task it hath to say:
That in the dreadful dead of dark midnight,
With shining cutlass, in my chamber crept
A skulking creature with a fiery torch,
Who softly cried 'Thou Roman dame, awake,
And entertain my love; else lasting shame
On thee and thine this night I will inflict.'
With this, I did begin to start and cry;
And then against my heart he sets his sword,
Swearing, unless I took all patiently,
I should not live to speak another word.
Mine enemy was strong, my poor self weak,
And far the weaker with so strong a fear.
My bloody judge forbade my voice to plead;
No rightful plea might sue for justice there.
O, speak, dear lord, my loving husband, speak:
How may this forcèd stain be wiped from me?
The poison'd fountain clears itself again;
And why not I from this compellèd blot?
O, teach me how to make mine own excuse!
Or at the least this refuge let me take:
Though my gross flesh with this abuse be smear'd,
Immaculate and spotless is my mind.
And therefore, for my sake, I do entreat,
For she that was Lucrece, your pristine wife,
Be suddenly revengèd on my foe.
The help that thou shalt lend comes all too late,
Yet let the traitor die, as is his fate.

*(As she exits, silhouetted in the projection screen, we see LUCRECE
unsheathe a dagger, and bring the point to her heart.)*

Exit LUCRECE.

HENRY
Oh...

JOHN
What?

HENRY
I've been looking for this...

JOHN
Who is it?

HENRY
Queen Elizabeth.

JOHN
From *The Life and Death of Queen Elizabeth*?

HENRY
Exactly.

[PROJECTION: A Field in Tilbury, Near the Mouth of the Thames River, 1588]

JOHN
Which speech is that?

HENRY
The famous speech at Tilbury...

JOHN
Near the mouth of the Thames...

HENRY
Rousing her troops to resist the Spanish Armada...

JOHN
Now sailing full force towards English shores...

(JOHN and HENRY flank the QUEEN and stand at attention as royal guards.)

QUEEN ELIZABETH
My loving people, we have been persuaded
By some who would be careful of our safety
To heed how we commit our royal presence
To armèd multitudes for fear of treachery;
But I assure you, I do not desire
To live to doubt my faithful, loving people.
Let tyrants fear; for I have always so
Behaved myself, that, under God, I've placed
My chiefest safeguard in the loyal hearts
And goodwill of my worthy subjects. Therefore,
I come amongst you at this perilous hour,
Not as a recreation or a sport,
But being resolved, i' th' midst and heat of battle,
To live or die amongst you; to lay down,
Not only for my God and for my kingdom,
But for my people, my honor and my blood,
Even the dust. I know I but possess
The body of a weak and feeble woman;
Yet herein beats the heart-blood of a king,
And of a king of England, too; and think
Unmitigable scorn that Spain or Parma,
Or any prince of Europe, dare invade
The borders of my sacred realms: to which,
Rather than countenance such foul dishonor
Should grow by me, myself will take up arms;
Myself will be your general and judge,
Rewarding all your virtues in the field.
I know already, by your forwardness,
That you have well deserved rewards and crowns;
And we do well assure you, by this hand,
They shall be duly paid you. In the mean,
Not doubting of your valor in the field,

We shortly shall obtain a famous victory
Over the enemies of God, of England,
And of my loving and devoted people.

(We hear the soldiers cheering.)

Exit QUEEN ELIZABETH.

JOHN
Is that all of it?

HENRY
I think so.

JOHN
So...? What should we do with them?

HENRY
Not sure.

(Pause. They survey the papers, now scattered everywhere.)

JOHN
Well...

HENRY
Let's decide tomorrow.

JOHN
Okay...

HENRY
Time for an ale?

JOHN
Absolutely.

HENRY
To the tavern!

JOHN
To the tavern!

(JOHN and HENRY blow out all the candles—except a single taper near the front door that JOHN forgets. They exit to the pub, leaving the papers behind.)

(A very brief silence.)

(We hear a door open as JOHN and HENRY re-enter abruptly.)

HENRY
Almost forgot!

JOHN
Forgot what?

(HENRY retrieves the First Folio from the box.)

HENRY
Let's show it off.

JOHN
Good idea!

(JOHN and HENRY exit again, with HENRY carrying the First Folio. We hear the door close.

The vibration from the door knocks over the last lit candle!

On the projection screens, we see the flames from the fallen candle spread from screen to screen until the room is engulfed. The sound of the fire grows, until we hear the conflagration consuming the entire building...

Then we begin to see the silhouettes of the women appearing among the flames—first one, then two, then more, crossing in both directions...

As the fire burns on, the women enter the stage from behind the screens, standing to face the audience in stark silhouette, backlit by the flames...

Suddenly, a burst of light briefly illuminates the faces of the women as we hear the sickening sound of an axe fall.

Blackout.)

[PROJECTION for Curtain Call: Finis]

END OF PLAY

INDEX OF SPEECHES

ALSO BY SCOTT KAISER

Now This

Splittin' the Raft

Love's Labor's Won

The Tao of Shakespeare

Shakespeare's Wordcraft

Mastering Shakespeare:
An Acting Class in Seven Scenes